COLLECTOR'S
VALUE GUIDE™

Fifty
State Quarters™

Complete Collection 1999-2008

"Old coins worn with finger-marks.
They tell stories."
— from "Street Window" by poet Carl Sandburg

This publication is *not* affiliated with the United States Mint or any of its affiliates, subsidiaries, distributors or representatives. Any opinions expressed are solely those of the authors, and do not necessarily reflect those of the United States Mint. "50 State Quarters" is a trademark of the United States Mint. Coin and bill designs are the property of the United States Mint. Some artwork has been provided courtesy of the Museum of the American Numismatic Association and these photos are the copyrighted property of the Museum of the American Numismatic Association.

Managing Editor:	Jeff Mahony	Creative Director:	Joe T. Nguyen
Associate Editors:	Melissa A. Bennett	Production Supervisor:	Scott Sierakowski
	Jan Cronan	Senior Graphic Designers:	Lance Doyle
	Gia C. Manalio		Susannah C. Judd
	Paula Stuckart		David S. Maloney
Contributing Editor:	Mike Micciulla		Carole Mattia-Slater
Editorial Assistants:	Jennifer Filipek	Graphic Designers:	Jennifer J. Bennett
	Nicole LeGard Lenderking		Sean-Ryan Dudley
	Joan C. Wheal		Kimberly Eastman
Research Assistants:	Timothy R. Affleck		Jason C. Jasch
	Heather N. Carreiro		Angi Shearstone
	Beth Hackett		David Ten Eyck
	Steven Shinkaruk	Art Interns:	Huy Hoang
Web Reporters:	Samantha Bouffard		Anna Zagajewska
	Ren Messina	Web Graphic Designer:	Ryan Falis
Editorial Intern:	Dan Ten Eyck	Product Development Manager:	Paul Rasid
		R&D Specialist:	Priscilla Berthiaume

ISBN 1-888-914-94-7

CheckerBee
PUBLISHING
306 Industrial Park Road • Middletown, CT 06457
www.collectorbee.com

Table Of Contents

Introducing The Collector's Value Guide™

Welcome to the Collector's Value Guide™ to the Fifty State Quarters! This handbook, along with the companion coin album, serves as your source for everything you need to know about this 10-year program.

So what's the story behind these exciting new quarters that have us all scrutinizing our loose change? Our handbook will show you how the program became a bill, then a law and ultimately real coins in your pocket. We will give you information on how the designs are chosen for each state, and how you can submit your own design for your home state.

We'll also make you familiar with and give you the stories behind the newest introductions in United States money, which include the new $5 and $10 bill designs and the Golden Dollar featuring Sacagawea, as well as the first 10 quarters in the State Quarters program.

Then we're on to a tour of our great nation as we give you trivia and fun facts about the 50 states and room to record which coins you have and where and when you received them.

We will also help you start a coin collection of your own by introducing you to some rare coins that are no longer in circulation, as well as some current favorites that can be found in your pockets right now. We'll advise you on what qualities to look for when collecting coins, and how to store your collection and keep it looking its best.

Then step into the U.S. Mint with us and discover what goes into the making of each coin!

In short, the Collector's Value Guide™ to the Fifty State Quarters is your definitive source for everything you need to get started in coin collecting. Happy hunting!

4

The Birth Of The State Quarters Program

Just what are those different quarters that keep ending up in your pocket change? Why are you seeing fewer and fewer quarters with eagles on them? When is your state's quarter coming out? Read on to learn more.

Since its debut in 1999, the Fifty State Quarters program has become one of the hottest collecting sensations in the country. The program, which is scheduled to release 50 quarters representing each state over a period of 10 years, has both adults and children pouring through their pocket change and has led to record-setting sales for the U.S. Mint.

KERMIT JUMPS AT THE CHANCE TO TELL STORY OF COINS

Kermit the Frog was named the official "spokesfrog" for the Fifty State Quarters program on June 3, 1999. Chosen because of his superb storytelling ability, which is key in telling the story of our nation's history, Kermit appears in both print and broadcast commercials to raise public awareness of the Fifty State Quarters program.

The program began as a bill introduced by Delaware Congressman Michael Castle, Chairman of the House Banking Subcommittee, which oversees U.S. coins. Mr. Castle and the members of Congress felt that having each state represented pictorially on a quarter would increase awareness of our country's diverse geography, history and heritage among both children and adults. The quarter was chosen for the program because it is the largest coin denomination in broad circulation and its large size provides a broad canvas for the designs.

President Bill Clinton agreed with the idea, and signed The 50 States Commemorative Coin Program Act into effect on December 1, 1997.

In accordance with the program, the U.S. Mint will release five new designs on the quarter annually, with a new design released every 10 weeks from 1999 through 2008. Once each quarter has finished its 10-week minting run, production of that quarter is stopped and production of the next quarter begins. The State Quarters are being released in the order in which the states ratified the Constitution and joined the Union. In 1999, the first five State Quarters (Delaware, Pennsylvania, New Jersey, Georgia and Connecticut) were released. A full schedule of releases can be found in the sidebar on page 9.

The Fifty State Quarters program marks the first time that we have strayed from the traditional quarter design since the 1976 Bicentennial Quarter, which was produced in honor of our country's 200th birthday

and featured a drummer boy. The U.S. Mint has stopped production of the eagle-design quarter, which features a profile of George Washington on the obverse and an American eagle on the reverse, but plans to return to producing it in 2009 after the Fifty State Quarters program concludes.

The Selection Process

The final design for each State Quarter is ultimately chosen by the U.S. Mint, but each state has a tremendous impact on its respective design. Approximately 18 months before the beginning of the year in which each state is to be honored, the U.S. Mint sends precise program guidelines to each state's governor. Among the guidelines is the instruction that no head-and-shoulders portrait or bust of any deceased person can appear on the coin. Also unacceptable is any design that portrays a still-living person. Additional restrictions are placed on commercial or private logos, and organizations that do not have universal membership or ownership.

The governor then appoints a liaison between the state and the U.S. Mint (often in the form of a multi-member committee) and asks state residents to submit their ideas for the state's quarter design to the

committee. Some states, such as Massachusetts, have limited their entrants to schoolchildren, and some, like Connecticut, have limited the ideas to one specific theme. Others, including New Hampshire, have opened the submission process to non-state residents. Georgia's governor delegated the task of developing concept ideas to the Georgia Council for the Arts. New Jersey took the same approach, with the 15-member New Jersey Commemorative Coin Design Commission taking responsibility for design conception.

The committee then chooses at least three, and no more than five, ideas as finalists for the quarter and sends them to the U.S. Mint for approval.

The U.S. Mint solicits opinions from two groups. The first is the Citizens Commemorative Coin Advisory Committee, a seven-member group made up of one representative from the U.S. Mint, three people from the numismatic community and three individuals from the general public. The second is the U.S. Fine Arts Commission, a seven-member, independent agency that advises the government on matters of national art and architecture. Together, the groups select three or four appropriate ideas to be turned into renderings of the coin design.

The Secretary of the Treasury then reviews and approves the designs and sends them back to the governor. The governor has the responsibility of selecting the final design, but often seeks input from state residents via Internet voting sites or special phone-in voting processes. The winning design is then sent back to the U.S. Mint one last time for final approval.

The Production Process

The State Quarters will be produced at two branches of the U.S. Mint: Denver and Philadelphia. This results in two different versions of each State Quarter. A small *P* or *D* that

indicates which U.S. Mint made the quarter can be found under the words "In God We Trust" on the obverse of the quarter. Therefore, a total of 100 State Quarters will

be circulated for the next 10 years.

In addition, the San Francisco Mint will produce proof versions (coins that do not go into circulation) of each of the quarters. These coins are stamped with an *S* to indicate their minting location. Many collectors choose to purchase uncirculated proof coins because they lack the marks and scratches sometimes found on circulated quarters.

Impact On Coin Collecting

The impact of the Fifty State Quarters program is twofold. In addition to promoting pride and education in our nation's heritage and geography, the program has injected new enthusiasm into the hobby of coin collecting. The U.S. Mint estimates that nearly 110 million U.S. residents are collecting the quarters, a number that is expected to increase to 160 million in the years ahead.

The popularity of the quarters as a collectible item is astounding. Philip Diehl, the director of the U.S. Mint, has said that the State Quarters have sold 100 times the

number that Pokémon cards have sold.

ARE MORE SPECIAL QUARTERS ON THE HORIZON?

On April 1, 1998, Congresswoman Eleanor Holmes-Norton of Washington, D.C. introduced a bill to create five future quarter releases to honor the District of Columbia and the U.S. territories of American Samoa, Guam, Puerto Rico and the U.S. Virgin Islands. This proposal, which would add one year to the quarters program, was still under consideration at press time.

Because so many collectors remove coins from circulation and place them in their collections, causing quarter shortages in certain areas, the U.S. Mint has increased the number of quarters they produce. There were 750 million of each of the first four quarters produced, but that figure has increased to one billion for each of the subsequent quarters.

To date, demand for the quarters has exceeded expectations. In one day, shortly after the Connecticut quarter made its debut, the U.S. Mint sold over $2 million worth of quarters and related products! The U.S. Mint estimates that their profit from sales of the quarters will reach approximately $5 billion by the end of the 10-year program. These profits will go to the U.S. Treasury's general fund for the support of its operations and programs. With the success of the program thus far, however, it would not be surprising if profits were even more substantial than anticipated.

Despite all the quarters that are being removed from circulation by collectors, there are more than enough for everyone. In addition to the many that are rotated in

State Quarters Release Dates

1999	2004
Delaware	Michigan
Pennsylvania	Florida
New Jersey	Texas
Georgia	Iowa
Connecticut	Wisconsin
2000	**2005**
Massachusetts	California
Maryland	Minnesota
South Carolina	Oregon
New Hampshire	Kansas
Virginia	West Virginia
2001	**2006**
New York	Nevada
North Carolina	Nebraska
Rhode Island	Colorado
Vermont	North Dakota
Kentucky	South Dakota
2002	**2007**
Tennessee	Montana
Ohio	Washington
Louisiana	Idaho
Indiana	Wyoming
Mississippi	Utah
2003	**2008**
Illinois	Oklahoma
Alabama	New Mexico
Maine	Arizona
Missouri	Alaska
Arkansas	Hawaii

everyday life as pocket change, special sets can be purchased through the U.S. Mint. Five-quarter sets are available each year and a complete set of all 50 quarters will be available at the end of the program. Proof sets, displays and bags filled with State Quarters are also available through the U.S. Mint.

The Fifty State Quarters program has proven to be a winning idea because in addition to bringing some excitement to coin collecting, it is an easy and educational hobby that instills a sense of national pride in all of us.

How To Submit Your Own Quarter Design

Here's how to submit your idea for your state's quarter design:

1. Log onto the U.S. Mint's web site, *www.usmint.gov*.

2. Click on the section "Find Out How To Submit A Design For Your State."

3. Read the instructions. You may want to print them out for future reference.

4. Download the "Blank Quarter Reverse Template" using the file format that works best for your computer.

5. Print out the template and create your own design in the space provided.

6. Send the completed template, along with your name, phone number and address to your state governor.

You may want to call your state governor's office before submitting your design, in case there are specific rules that you should follow.

The First 10 State Quarters

All 50 states won't be represented on the State Quarters until 2008, but we do know the designs of the first 10 quarters to be circulated. Here is some background into how and why the selected designs were chosen, and how each of the designs relates to its corresponding state.

Delaware

Quarter Release Date: January 1999

Delaware's quarter design features Caesar Rodney on horseback. The quarter also has the words 'The First State," which is Delaware's nickname.

Rodney was a member of Delaware's delegation to the Continental Congress, which was meeting in Philadelphia in July of 1776 to vote on declaring independence from England. The other two Delaware delegates, Thomas McKean and George Read, were deadlocked as to their decision, so Rodney was called upon to break the tie. Although quite ill from cancer and suffering from asthma, he rode 80 miles from Dover, Delaware to Philadelphia on horseback in the oppressive summer heat and sometimes-violent thunderstorms to cast his vote for independence.

The Rodney State Quarter was designed by Eddy Seger, a drama and art teacher at Caesar Rodney High School in Camden-Wyoming, Delaware. Seger's was among the 300 designs submitted to the Delaware Arts Council in response to a call for submissions by Governor Thomas R. Carper in February of 1998.

Caesar Rodney rides into circulation

Pennsylvania

Quarter Release Date: March 1999

"Commonwealth" stands heads above the rest

The governor of Pennsylvania, Tom Ridge, chose a quarter design that would educate the public about the founding principles of the Keystone State. Highlighting the coin is the statue of "Commonwealth," a female figure who serves as an allegorical representation of the Commonwealth of Pennsylvania. Designed by sculptor Roland Hinton Perry, "Commonwealth" has stood atop Pennsylvania's capitol dome since May 25, 1905. The statue's right arm is extended in mercy, while her left hand is holding a ribboned mace that represents justice.

A keystone also figures in the quarter design, representative of the state's nickname and Pennsylvania's key position in the development of the federal union. The state motto "Virtue, Liberty, Independence" is the third element in the design, and is in the background with the outline of Pennsylvania.

Runner-up designs included a quarter featuring the motto and the state bird, the Ruffed Grouse, the state flower, the Mountain Laurel, and the state tree, the Hemlock; a design that utilized the keystone as its central image, framed by the state bird and flower; and a contender that portrayed a Lenape Indian chieftain and William Penn shaking hands over a treaty and a peace pipe. This design also included the keystone and outline of the state along with the inscription "Penn's Woods."

New Jersey

Quarter Release Date: May 1999

The New Jersey quarter design is a representation of the Emmanuel Leutze painting "Washington Crossing the Delaware." At the bottom of the coin are the words "Crossroads Of The Revolution," New Jersey's slogan during the United States Bicentennial celebration in 1976.

On a bitterly cold Christmas night in 1776, General George Washington and his troops crossed the Delaware River into New Jersey on their way to eventual victories against the British. The Revolutionary War battles of Trenton and Princeton won New Jersey back from the British, who retreated to New York. More than 200 battles were fought in New Jersey during the Revolutionary War, truly making it the "Crossroads of the Revolution."

Leutze was born in Germany in 1816 and immigrated to the United States as a child, settling in Philadelphia. He returned to Germany in 1840 to study the art of painting, but sent a number of his paintings to the United States. He painted mainly renderings of English and American historical episodes. "Washington Crossing the Delaware" now hangs in the Metropolitan Museum of Art in New York City.

There were two other designs considered for the New Jersey State Quarter. The first one portrayed Barnegat Lighthouse and inlet, with the New Jersey state motto, "Liberty and Prosperity," engraved to the left of the image. The other featured an outline of the state, George Washington on his steed directing his troops and Barnegat Lighthouse in the background.

Leutze's "Crossing" comes to life

Georgia

Quarter Release Date: July 1999

Georgia chooses a "peach" of a design

Commonly known as "The Peach State," Georgia has a reputation for delivering the nation's plumpest, juiciest and tastiest peaches. The crop is an economic staple for Georgia, and in 1995 the peach was designated as Georgia's official state fruit.

So it is no surprise that the peach takes center stage on the Georgia quarter. It is situated within an outline of the state, and a banner draped over the outline proclaims the state's motto of "Wisdom, Justice, Moderation." This motto, which is borrowed from the Constitution, embodies the traditional ideals of the state. The design is bordered on the right and left by sprigs of Live Oak, representing Georgia's state tree. Governor Roy Barnes said the coin "perfectly depicts the grace and beauty of our state."

Several other designs were considered for the Georgia quarter. One showcased the state outline, with the capital of Atlanta identified by a star. The Brown Thrasher and the Cherokee Rose, the state bird and flower, also appeared on this coin design. Another design again featured the peach, state outline and motto, this time with a Cherokee Rose border. The final contender showed the state outline with "Hope" written inside it along with symbols of education and recreation. A sun, its rays beaming on the state, appeared to the upper right of the state outline.

Connecticut

Quarter Release Date: October 1999

The oak tree pictured on the Connecticut quarter played a vital role in Connecticut's history. In 1662, Charles II of Britain granted Connecticut a charter that proclaimed it an independent Colonial government. Under King James II, however, Connecticut's charter was challenged and in 1687, that king sent a representative to Connecticut to demand the surrender of the charter.

The story goes that representatives of the colony were engaged in a heated discussion with the King's representative, the Connecticut charter on the table between them, when the candles illuminating the room suddenly went out. When the candles were relit, the charter had disappeared. It turned out that Captain Joseph Wadsworth had hidden it in a nearby oak tree – a tree soon named the Charter Oak.

Although the tree was eventually destroyed during an 1856 storm, saplings were taken from it, so the Charter Oak still grows today.

Andy Jones, a teacher of art at Eastern Connecticut State University in Willimantic, designed the image that appears on the Connecticut quarter.

The other two designs that were considered for the Connecticut quarter also featured renditions of the Charter Oak. One depicted the tree in full leafy bloom with the words "The Charter Oak" beneath it. The other featured an image of the Connecticut Charter before a more stylized rendition of the Charter Oak.

The legend of the Charter Oak lives on

Massachusetts

Quarter Release Date: January 2000

Minuteman makes his way in State Quarter program

The Revolutionary War soldier, the minuteman, is the prominent feature on the Massachusetts quarter. Minutemen were elite Revolutionary War soldiers who were selected for their ability to prepare for battle in a "minute" in their endeavors to defend the colonies. The minuteman is shown standing in front of an outline of the state, which has a star indicating the state's capital, Boston. The state's nickname "The Bay State" completes the coin. The pilgrims came ashore at the Massachusetts Bay town of Plymouth, and the port city of Boston is located on Massachusetts Bay.

Xander Kotsatos, who was a fifth-grader attending the Belmont Day School at the time he submitted his design, and Kathleen Raughtigan, who was in fourth grade at St. Bernard's in Fitchburg at the time of the contest, submitted separate but similar entries to the Massachusetts quarter design contest and are named co-artists of the design. Xander also considered the *U.S.S. Constitution* or the *Mayflower* for his design, but felt that the minuteman better represented the entire state. Kathleen chose the minuteman for her design because her classmates were submitting suggestions of the state bird and flower, and she wanted to do something different.

The Revolutionary War battleship the *U.S.S. Constitution* (affectionately known as "Old Ironsides") and the first lighthouse built in the United States, the Boston Light, were also design candidates. Both of these treasures from Boston's history stand today and are frequent tourist destinations.

Maryland

Quarter Release Date: March 2000

The dome of Maryland's state house in Annapolis is at the forefront of Maryland's quarter design. The honor is well deserved, as the landmark is not only the oldest working state house in the United States, but it also once served as the U.S. Capitol Building. Furthermore, its dome is the largest wooden structure of its kind in North America.

This rendition of the state house is surrounded by White Oak leaves (the leaves of the state tree) and one of the state's slogans, "The Old Line State." This phrase was coined by George Washington during the Revolutionary War. Washington fought with the First Maryland Regiment to defend New York against the British. Impressed by the soldiers' abilities, he named them the "old line" to reflect their talents. Incidentally, this slogan was not well known to many residents before it was announced that it would appear on the quarter.

The quarter was designed by William Krawczewicz, a White House graphic artist from Crofton, Maryland. Krawczewicz submitted seven suggestions for Maryland's quarter design. Three of them made it through the first cut and two of them (the ships the *Ark* and the *Dove,* which brought the first colonists to Maryland, and the winning design) were in the final round of choices. Krawczewicz has plenty of experience in coin designing, as he formerly worked for the U.S. Mint and designed several commemorative coins.

"Old Line State" boasts oldest working state house (artist's rendition)

South Carolina

Quarter Release Date: May 2000

Palmetto tree is more than just beautiful
(artist's rendition)

The South Carolina quarter unites the state's symbols in a tribute to the state's natural beauty. The Palmetto tree represents the state's strength, as the tree's wood was used to make bunkers for Revolutionary War soldiers during the battle at Fort Moultrie. The spongy wood absorbed the bullets and cannonballs from the British Red Coats, thereby saving the lives of the American soldiers and preserving the safety of the fort.

The Carolina Wren, the state bird, is representative of the state's southern hospi-tality and the state flower, the Yellow Jessamine, is representative of the state's natural beauty.

According to South Carolina governor Jim Hodges, "These three state emblems symbolize what is best about South Carolina." An outline of the state with a star marking the state capital of Columbia, and the state's nickname, "The Palmetto State," complete the design.

The two other images in contention for the South Carolina State Quarter were the state house and a scene from the previous-ly mentioned battle at Fort Moultrie. The battle took place on Sullivans Island on June 28, 1776 and was the first decisive mil-itary victory of the American Revolution. The scene depicted Sgt. William Jasper re-raising the flag of Fort Moultrie's in triumph after it had been shot down by the British. The words "Fort Moultrie" were also embla-zoned on this design.

New Hampshire

Quarter Release Date: July 2000

New Hampshire's quarter design incorporates the state's beauty and history of independent thought and action.

The "Old Man of the Mountain" is a natural rock formation jutting out from the side of Cannon Mountain in Franconia Notch State Park, which is part of the White Mountain National Forest. "The Profile," as it is sometimes called, is formed by five granite ledges that give the impression of a man's profile. It is a natural landmark that is both familiar to, and loved by, New Hampshire residents. The "Old Man of the Mountain" inspired American author Nathaniel Hawthorne's short story "The Great Stone Face."

The state's motto, "Live Free or Die," was originally uttered by General John Stark, the hero of the Battle of Bennington during the Revolutionary War. The highly regarded Stark was asked to speak at the 32nd anniversary celebration of the Battle of Bennington, which he was unable to attend. Instead, he sent this message to his former comrades: "Live free or die. Death is not the worst of evils." Years later, the first four words of this sentiment were adopted by New Hampshire as its state motto.

The nine stars on the coin represent New Hampshire's place as the ninth of the original 13 colonies to join the Union. This is significant, as New Hampshire's vote for independence was the one that fulfilled the two-thirds vote requirement necessary to ratify the U.S. Constitution.

"Old Man of the Mountain" travels across the country on coin (artist's rendition)

Virginia

Quarter Release Date: October 2000

Anniversary celebration spreads to State Quarter (artist's rendition)

The State Quarter for Virginia depicts three 17th-century sailing ships and the words "Jamestown 1607-2007" and "Quadracentennial." The ships are the *Discovery, Susan Constant* and *Godspeed.* In 1607 they brought the first settlers to Jamestown and marked the beginning of Colonial history in America. The Jamestown area was the first permanent British colony in America and it and the entire state are eagerly anticipating the celebration of Jamestown's 400th anniversary in 2007.

Jamestown, which was named after England's King James I by its more than 100 colonists, played many other significant roles in American history as well. The first representative legislative assembly was held there in 1619, forming the basis for today's Virginia General Assembly, the oldest continuous legislative body in the United States. Jamestown also served as the capital of Virginia until 1699, at which time it was moved to Williamsburg.

Other candidates for the State Quarter design included a drawing of Virginia's state capitol building in Richmond, which was designed by Thomas Jefferson; a drawing of George Washington's home, Mount Vernon, overlooking the Potomac river and shown with Dogwood blossoms (which is both the state flower and the state tree); and the Colonial capital at Williamsburg.

The Golden Dollar

The United States Dollar Coin Act of 1997, signed in December of 1997 by President Bill Clinton, instructed the U.S. Treasury to place a new one-dollar coin into circulation to replace the depleted supply of Susan B. Anthony one-dollar coins. The new Golden Dollar bears the image of Sacagawea.

In early 2000, the U.S. Mint began releasing its first new one-dollar coin issued in 20 years, the Golden Dollar. This new coin features Sacagawea, the 15-year-old Shoshone Indian who served as guide and translator for Meriwether Lewis and William Clark during their 1804-1806 exploration of the American West. The American Bald Eagle graces the reverse side of the coin.

The U.S. Treasury dictated that the new coin had to feature a non-living woman on the obverse (heads) and an eagle, reflecting peace and freedom, on the reverse (tails).

A seven-member advisory committee chose to honor Sacagawea, and then solicited designs from 23 professional artists. More than 120 designs were submitted, and the public was invited to comment on them. On May 4, 1999, the U.S. Mint proudly unveiled the final design.

Sacagawea is shown in three-quarter profile, looking directly at the viewer (a first for a U.S. coin). She carries her son, Jean Baptiste, on her back. Sacagawea gave birth to Jean Baptiste early in her travels with Lewis and Clark. Her husband, fur trader Toussaint Charbonneau, also traveled with the group.

The eagle is encircled by 17 stars that represent the 17 states in the Union at the time of the Lewis and Clark expedition.

The Golden Dollar is the same size as the Susan B. Anthony coin (26.5 mm in diameter), has a smooth edge (like a nickel) and is golden in color. It is made of copper, zinc, manganese and nickel.

The New Excitement In U.S. Bill Designs

Since 1996, the United States Treasury has been issuing new currency notes designed with a number of extra security features to help protect against counterfeiting. The $5 and $10 bills are the latest to be changed.

The $5 bill features a portrait of Abraham Lincoln on the front and the Lincoln Memorial on the back. The $10 note features a portrait of the first Secretary of the Treasury, Alexander Hamilton, on the front and the U.S. Treasury Building on the reverse. Both of the newly designed denominations contain many new features.

The new notes incorporate a fine-line printing pattern behind the portraits and the buildings, making the notes extremely difficult to replicate. In addition, the portraits are very detailed, which makes duplication difficult. The portraits are off-centered to reduce wear and tear on the design.

Each bill has a new watermark, which mirrors the note's historical figure. When the bill is held up to a light, the watermark is visible from both sides.

A new official seal has been added to the left side of the front of each bill, while a new letter and number combination has been added directly below the bill's serial number. This letter and number combination identifies the issuing Federal Reserve bank that produced the bill (see page 57 for more information on the markings on bills). An extra letter has been added to the serial number to bring the total to eleven digits.

Each new bill now has a polymer security thread embedded vertically in the note.

This thread is located on the left side of the portrait on the $5 note and on the right side of the portrait on the $10 note. This thread glows blue on the $5 bill and white on the $10 bill when held under an ultraviolet light. The words *USA FIVE* or *USA TEN* and a flag with the number *5* or *10* can be found to the left of the portrait. As with the watermark, these features can be seen from both sides of the bill when held up to a bright light.

Another added security feature is the addition of microprinted words on the front of each bill, print that is so small that it is hard to duplicate. On the $5 note, *The United States of America* is repeated in microprint on the portrait's lower oval frame, while *FIVE DOLLARS* is repeated on both side borders of the bill. On the $10 note, *The United States of America* is repeated in microprint above Hamilton's name, while *TEN* is repeated inside the lower left-hand numeral.

The back of each bill contains a large numeral in the lower right-hand corner,

designed to make the note easier to read for both the visually impaired and the elderly. Both the $5 and $10 bills also include a machine-readable feature in the event that scanning devices are developed to help the blind identify these notes.

Unique to the $10 bill is the use of color-shifting ink on the number 10 in the lower left-hand corner of the reverse side. This makes the number look either green or black, depending on the angle from which it is viewed.

The new $5 and $10 notes are expected to gradually replace the original notes. In the meantime, the old bills will not face any devaluation or recall, and will still be accepted at full face value.

How To Use Your Quarter Record & State Reference Guide

Now that you've learned all about the Fifty State Quarters program, you may want to start collecting the State Quarters. This section of the book is designed to help you keep track of your State Quarters collection.

The following pages feature a write-in section to track your State Quarters collection. As you collect each quarter, record which version of the quarter you have (Philadelphia or Denver Mint), and where and when you got it.

These pages are dedicated to each of the 50 states and are filled with informa-tion. The maps of the states are marked with a star to denote the state capital and each state's flag is shown to the right of the fill-in section. The states are ranked by order of admission (first to last) and number of residents and area (largest to smallest). This information comes from *The World Almanac® And Book Of Facts 1999,* published by World Almanac Books.

Also included on these pages is all kinds of trivia, from each state's date of admission to the Union to such things as famous natives and interesting tourist destinations.

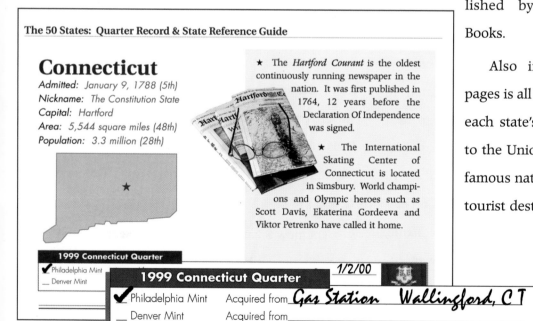

The 50 States: Quarter Record & State Reference Guide

Connecticut

Admitted: *January 9, 1788 (5th)*
Nickname: *The Constitution State*
Capital: *Hartford*
Area: *5,544 square miles (48th)*
Population: *3.3 million (28th)*

★ The *Hartford Courant* is the oldest continuously running newspaper in the nation. It was first published in 1764, 12 years before the Declaration Of Independence was signed.

★ The International Skating Center of Connecticut is located in Simsbury. World champions and Olympic heroes such as Scott Davis, Ekaterina Gordeeva and Viktor Petrenko have called it home.

1999 Connecticut Quarter

✓ Philadelphia Mint
__ Denver Mint   1/2/00

1999 Connecticut Quarter

✓ Philadelphia Mint   Acquired from *Gas Station   Wallingford, CT*   Date: *1/2/00*
__ Denver Mint   Acquired from_____   Date: _____

Alabama

Admitted: December 14, 1819 (22nd)

Nickname: The Heart of Dixie

Capital: Montgomery

Area: 52,237 square miles (30th)

Population: 4.3 million (23rd)

★ In 1965, Dr. Martin Luther King Jr. led thousands of protesters on a 49-mile march from Selma to Montgomery to advocate voting rights for blacks. Shortly thereafter, President Lyndon Johnson signed the Voting Rights Act .

★ Alabama-born track and field great Jesse Owens' finest moment came during the 1936 Berlin Olympics where, under the ominous presence of Adolf Hitler, he won four gold medals.

2003 Alabama Quarter

__ Philadelphia Mint   Acquired from_____   Date: _____

__ Denver Mint   Acquired from_____   Date: _____

Alaska

Admitted: January 3, 1959 (49th)

Nickname: The Last Frontier

Capital: Juneau

Area: 615,230 square miles (1st)

Population: 609,311 (48th)

★ The Alaska Bald Eagle Festival, held in Haines, celebrates the arrival of approximately 3,000 bald eagles that converge upon the nearby Chilkat River. The river quickly becomes the largest bald eagle gathering spot in the world.

★ Alaska is home to the largest oil field in the United States!

★ If you have what it takes to create a sculpture from a block of ice, pay a visit to the annual Fairbanks Ice Art Competition, held every March.

2008 Alaska Quarter

__ Philadelphia Mint   Acquired from_____   Date: _____

__ Denver Mint   Acquired from_____   Date: _____

Arizona

Admitted: February 14, 1912 (48th)
Nickname: The Grand Canyon State
Capital: Phoenix
Area: 114,006 square miles (6th)
Population: 4.6 million (21st)

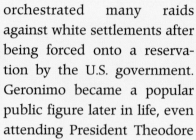

★ The mighty waters of the Colorado River continue to erode the walls of the Grand Canyon, a process that has been occurring for millions of years.

★ The Apache leader Geronimo was born in what is now Clifton in 1829. He orchestrated many raids against white settlements after being forced onto a reservation by the U.S. government. Geronimo became a popular public figure later in life, even attending President Theodore Roosevelt's inaugural procession.

2008 Arizona Quarter			
__ Philadelphia Mint	Acquired from_____	Date: _____	
__ Denver Mint	Acquired from_____	Date: _____	

Arkansas

Admitted: June 15, 1836 (25th)
Nickname: The Natural State
Capital: Little Rock
Area: 53,182 square miles (28th)
Population: 2.5 million (33rd)

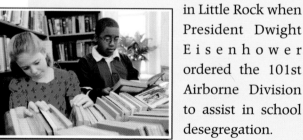

★ William Jefferson "Bill" Clinton, the 42nd President of the United States, was born in Hope in 1946. Elected in 1992, he became the first president born after World War II.

★ In 1957, African-American and white children finally attended school together in Little Rock when President Dwight Eisenhower ordered the 101st Airborne Division to assist in school desegregation.

2003 Arkansas Quarter			
__ Philadelphia Mint	Acquired from_____	Date: _____	
__ Denver Mint	Acquired from_____	Date: _____	

California

Admitted: September 9, 1850 (31st)
Nickname: The Golden State
Capital: Sacramento
Area: 158,869 square miles (3rd)
Population: 32.3 million (1st)

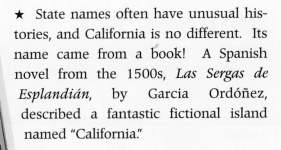

★ State names often have unusual histories, and California is no different. Its name came from a book! A Spanish novel from the 1500s, *Las Sergas de Esplandián*, by Garcia Ordóñez, described a fantastic fictional island named "California."

★ Baker has a thermometer that stands 134 feet tall. Billed as the world's tallest, this thermometer commemorates the 1913 event when the mercury rose to 134 degrees Fahrenheit at nearby Death Valley, the highest temperature ever recorded in the United States.

2005 California Quarter			
__ Philadelphia Mint	Acquired from_____	Date: _____	
__ Denver Mint	Acquired from_____	Date: _____	

Colorado

Admitted: August 1, 1876 (38th)
Nickname: The Centennial State
Capital: Denver
Area: 104,100 square miles (8th)
Population: 3.9 million (25th)

★ The sand dunes at Great Sand Dunes National Monument are the tallest in North America. They loom at heights of more than 700 feet above sea level.

★ The exterior of the capitol building's dome is covered in 24-karat gold, while

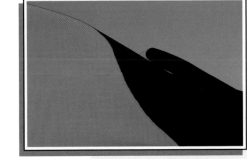

its interior is made of "Beulah Red" marble, of which there is no more in the world because it was all used on the dome.

2006 Colorado Quarter			
__ Philadelphia Mint	Acquired from_____	Date: _____	
__ Denver Mint	Acquired from_____	Date: _____	

Connecticut

Admitted: January 9, 1788 (5th)

Nickname: The Constitution State

Capital: Hartford

Area: 5,544 square miles (48th)

Population: 3.3 million (28th)

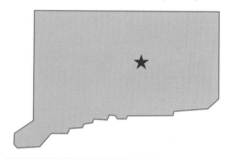

★ The *Hartford Courant* is the oldest continuously running newspaper in the nation. It was first published in 1764, 12 years before the Declaration Of Independence was signed.

★ The International Skating Center of Connecticut is located in Simsbury. World champions and Olympic heroes such as Scott Davis, Ekaterina Gordeeva and Viktor Petrenko have called it home.

1999 Connecticut Quarter

__ Philadelphia Mint	Acquired from_____	Date: _____
__ Denver Mint	Acquired from_____	Date: _____

Delaware

Admitted: December 7, 1787 (1st)

Nickname: The First State

Capital: Dover

Area: 2,396 square miles (49th)

Population: 731,581 (46th)

★ Speeds can get as fast as 150 miles per hour at the Dover Downs International Speedway. Located in the heart of the capital city of Dover, the so-called "Monster Mile" is one of NASCAR's premier tracks in the Mid-Atlantic.

★ Delaware is named after Sir Thomas West, Baron De La Warr, Virginia's first governor. His name is also the namesake of the Delaware River and the Delaware Bay.

1999 Delaware Quarter

__ Philadelphia Mint	Acquired from_____	Date: _____
__ Denver Mint	Acquired from_____	Date: _____

Florida

Admitted: March 3, 1845 (27th)
Nickname: The Sunshine State
Capital: Tallahassee
Area: 59,928 square miles (23rd)
Population: 14.7 million (4th)

★ Florida's Pelican Island has the honor of being the country's first National Wildlife Refuge. Established in 1903, Pelican Island covers more than 5,000 acres and is home to nearly 100 species of birds and other threatened or endangered animals.

★ St. Augustine, in northern Florida, is the oldest city in the United States. It was founded by the Spanish explorer Don Pedro Menendez de Aviles in 1565 .

2004 Florida Quarter			
__ Philadelphia Mint	Acquired from_____	Date: _____	
__ Denver Mint	Acquired from_____	Date: _____	

Georgia

Admitted: January 1, 1788 (4th)
Nickname: The Peach State
Capital: Atlanta
Area: 58,977 square miles (24th)
Population: 7.5 million (10th)

★ James Earl "Jimmy" Carter Jr., the 39th president of the United States, was born in Plains on October 1, 1924.

★ Born in Atlanta in 1929, Martin Luther King Jr. was a prominent civil rights leader of the 1950s and 1960s. King organized peaceful protests including the Montgomery bus boycott and a march on Washington, D.C. He was assassinated on April 4, 1968 while in Memphis, Tennessee supporting striking sanitation workers.

1999 Georgia Quarter			
__ Philadelphia Mint	Acquired from_____	Date: _____	
__ Denver Mint	Acquired from_____	Date: _____	

Hawaii

Admitted: August 21, 1959 (50th)
Nickname: The Aloha State
Capital: Honolulu
Area: 6,459 square miles (47th)
Population: 1.2 million (41st)

★ The wettest spot on Earth is Mount Waialeale, on the island of Kauai. It averages almost 500 inches of rain annually.

★ The active volcano Mauna Loa, on the island of Hawaii, is the world's largest volcanic mass, rising 13,680 feet above sea level, with much of its mass underwater. As much of Mauna Loa is underwater, its true height is much greater.

2008 Hawaii Quarter			
__ Philadelphia Mint	Acquired from_____	Date: _____	
__ Denver Mint	Acquired from_____	Date: _____	

Idaho

Admitted: July 3, 1890 (43rd)
Nickname: The Gem State
Capital: Boise
Area: 83,574 square miles (14th)
Population: 1.2 million (40th)

★ In 1860s Idaho, towns sprang up everywhere to mine the rich lodes of gold, silver and other precious metals. The town of Silver City, once a prosperous mining town, is now a community of abandoned buildings and six people!

★ Most of us think "Hawaii" when we hear about volcanoes. But Craters of the Moon National Monument, 1600 square miles of craters and cones formed by volcanoes, is located in Idaho.

2007 Idaho Quarter			
__ Philadelphia Mint	Acquired from_____	Date: _____	
__ Denver Mint	Acquired from_____	Date: _____	

Illinois

Admitted: December 3, 1818 (21st)

Nickname: The Prairie State

Capital: Springfield

Area: 57,918 square miles (25th)

Population: 11.9 million (6th)

★ Chicago is home to the first skyscraper ever built. Architect William LeBaron Jenney unveiled the nine-story Home Insurance Building in 1885.

★ In 1899 Ernest Hemingway was born in Oak Park. He would go on to fame as a reporter, adventurer and Nobel Prize-winning author.

★ Although he was born in Kentucky, Abraham Lincoln was raised in New Salem, Illinois, leading to one of the state's nicknames, "Land of Lincoln."

2003 Illinois Quarter			
__ Philadelphia Mint	Acquired from_____	Date: _____	
__ Denver Mint	Acquired from_____	Date: _____	

Indiana

Admitted: December 11, 1816 (19th)

Nickname: The Hoosier State

Capital: Indianapolis

Area: 36,420 square miles (38th)

Population: 5.9 million (14th)

★ If you like covered bridges, you'll feel right at home in Parke County. It is home to 32 of them, earning the county the title "The Covered Bridge Capital."

★ He was the Boston Celtics' Most Valuable Player 3 years in a row, an NBA All-Star 12 times, and a member of the 1992 U.S. Olympic basketball team. But once upon a time, Larry Bird, was just a kid growing up in French Lick.

2002 Indiana Quarter			
__ Philadelphia Mint	Acquired from_____	Date: _____	
__ Denver Mint	Acquired from_____	Date: _____	

Iowa

Admitted: December 28, 1846 (29th)
Nickname: The Hawkeye State
Capital: Des Moines
Area: 56,276 square miles (26th)
Population: 2.9 million (30th)

★ Intrigued by the life of a hobo? You can find out about this colorful lifestyle at the National Hobo Convention, held every year in Britt.

★ When Peru farmer Jesse Hiatt first encountered a strange variety of apples in his field, he wanted to get rid of them. But nearly a century later, those Red Delicious apples are loved the world over.

2004 Iowa Quarter			
__ Philadelphia Mint	Acquired from_____	Date: _____	
__ Denver Mint	Acquired from_____	Date: _____	

Kansas

Admitted: January 29, 1861 (34th)
Nickname: The Sunflower State
Capital: Topeka
Area: 82,282 square miles (15th)
Population: 2.6 million (32nd)

★ In 1950 Reverend Oliver Brown's child was turned away from a Topeka public school. Brown began a class-action suit against the local board of education that went all the way to the Supreme Court. The landmark 1954 decision of Brown v. Board of Education put an end to "separate but equal" education.

★ David F. McFarland and H.P. Cady discovered helium at the University of Kansas in 1903.

2005 Kansas Quarter			
__ Philadelphia Mint	Acquired from_____	Date: _____	
__ Denver Mint	Acquired from_____	Date: _____	

Kentucky

Admitted: June 1, 1792 (15th)
Nickname: The Bluegrass State
Capital: Frankfort
Area: 40,411 square miles (37th)
Population: 3.9 million (24th)

★ Mammoth Cave, part of Mammoth Cave National Park, has more than 350 miles of passageways and is known as the world's longest cave system.

★ The Kentucky Derby, held every year since 1875 at Louisville's Churchill Downs, is the oldest continuously held horse race in the country.

★ Abraham Lincoln was born on February 12, 1809 near what is now Hodgenville.

2001 Kentucky Quarter

☐ Philadelphia Mint   Acquired from_____ Date: _____
☐ Denver Mint   Acquired from_____ Date: _____

Louisiana

Admitted: April 30, 1812 (18th)
Nickname: The Pelican State
Capital: Baton Rouge
Area: 49,651 square miles (31st)
Population: 4.4 million (22nd)

★ The world's longest boxing match was held in New Orleans on April 6, 1893. The match went 110 rounds and lasted 7 hours and 19 minutes before a draw was called.

★ New Orleans is home to the famous Mardi Gras carnival, a 12-day celebration of music, parades and parties that culminates on Fat Tuesday, the day before the start of Lent. *Fat Tuesday* is the direct translation of the French Mardi Gras.

2002 Louisiana Quarter

☐ Philadelphia Mint   Acquired from_____ Date: _____
☐ Denver Mint   Acquired from_____ Date: _____

Maine

Admitted: March 15, 1820 (23rd)
Nickname: The Pine Tree State
Capital: Augusta
Area: 33,741 square miles (39th)
Population: 1.2 million (39th)

★ Maine is famous for lobster, and with good reason — Maine fisherman typically catch half the nation's lobster supply.

★ The city of Farmington holds a Chester Greenwood Day celebration each year in honor of its native son who invented earmuffs in 1877.

★ Poet Henry Wadsworth Longfellow was born in Portland in 1807. His childhood home is a popular site for tourists to visit.

2003 Maine Quarter

☐ Philadelphia Mint Acquired from_____ Date:_____
☐ Denver Mint Acquired from_____ Date:_____

Maryland

Admitted: April 28, 1788 (7th)
Nickname: The Old Line State
Capital: Annapolis
Area: 12,297 square miles (42nd)
Population: 5.1 million (19th)

★ Fort McHenry National Monument in Baltimore commemorates the place where, in 1814, Francis Scott Key was inspired to write the words to "The Star-Spangled Banner."

★ Jousting is the official state sport of Maryland. Jousting tournaments are held during the summer months

★ Babe Ruth was born in Baltimore in 1895 and is immortalized at the Babe Ruth Museum at Camden Yards.

2000 Maryland Quarter

☐ Philadelphia Mint Acquired from_____ Date:_____
☐ Denver Mint Acquired from_____ Date:_____

Massachusetts

Admitted: February 6, 1788 (6th)

Nickname: The Bay State

Capital: Boston

Area: 9,241 square miles (45th)

Population: 6.1 million (13th)

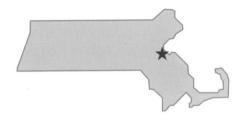

★ The sport of basketball was invented in Springfield by James A. Naismith in 1891. The Baskeball Hall of Fame is located in Springfield.

★ The Minute Man National Historical Park is located in Lexington and Concord. It commemorates the battle between Minutemen and British troops, which launched the Revolutionary War on April 19, 1775 with the "shot heard around the world."

2000 Massachusetts Quarter			
☐ Philadelphia Mint	Acquired from_____	Date: _____	
☐ Denver Mint	Acquired from_____	Date: _____	

Michigan

Admitted: January 26, 1837 (26th)

Nickname: The Wolverine State

Capital: Lansing

Area: 96,705 square miles (11th)

Population: 9.8 million (8th)

★ Artists from all over the world travel to Plymouth each January to take part in the city's annual ice-sculpting festival.

★ Michigan contains more than 11,000 lakes. Its shores touch four of the five Great Lakes, giving rise to one of its nicknames, "The Great Lake State."

★ Battle Creek is known as the "Cereal Bowl of America," as it produces more cereal than any city in the world.

2004 Michigan Quarter			
☐ Philadelphia Mint	Acquired from_____	Date: _____	
☐ Denver Mint	Acquired from_____	Date: _____	

Minnesota

Admitted: May 11, 1858 (32nd)
Nickname: The Gopher State
Capital: St. Paul
Area: 86,943 square miles (12th)
Population: 4.7 million (20th)

★ Minnesota's climate is perfect for winter sports, so it's no wonder that the United States Hockey Hall of Fame is located in Eveleth.

★ Charles M. Schulz, creator of Charlie Brown, Snoopy, Linus, Lucy and the rest of the beloved "Peanuts" comic strip gang, was born in Minneapolis in 1922.

★ Can you imagine life without transparent cellophane tape? In 1930, the sticky stuff was invented and patented by Richard Drew of St. Paul.

2005 Minnesota Quarter

☐ Philadelphia Mint   Acquired from_____ Date: _____
☐ Denver Mint   Acquired from_____ Date: _____

Mississippi

Admitted: December 10, 1817 (20th)
Nickname: The Magnolia State
Capital: Jackson
Area: 48,286 square miles (32nd)
Population: 2.7 million (31st)

★ Visitors to Vicksburg can visit the Biedenharn Candy Company Museum, which commemorates the site where, in 1894, Coca-Cola was first bottled.

★ The world's first heart transplant, in which a human's heart was replaced with the heart of a chimpanzee, was performed in 1964 by Dr. James D. Hardy at the University of Mississippi Medical Center in Jackson.

2002 Mississippi Quarter

☐ Philadelphia Mint   Acquired from_____ Date: _____
☐ Denver Mint   Acquired from_____ Date: _____

Missouri

Admitted: August 10, 1821 (24th)
Nickname: The Show Me State
Capital: Jefferson City
Area: 69,709 square miles (21st)
Population: 5.4 million (16th)

★ The Gateway Arch in St. Louis symbolizes the city's role as the "Gateway to the West." At 630 feet high, it stands as the nation's tallest man-made monument.

★ Scientist George Washington Carver, famed for developing numerous industrial applications from agricultural products like peanuts and sweet potatoes, is commemorated at the George Washington Carver National Monument, located near Diamond.

2003 Missouri Quarter				
☐ Philadelphia Mint	Acquired from_____	Date: _____	
☐ Denver Mint	Acquired from_____	Date: _____	

Montana

Admitted: November 8, 1889 (41st)
Nickname: The Treasure State
Capital: Helena
Area: 147,046 square miles (4th)
Population: 878,810 (44th)

★ Little Bighorn Battlefield National Monument is the site where the Battle of Little Bighorn, also known as Custer's Last Stand, occurred in 1876. Cheyenne and Sioux warriors, led by Sitting Bull and Crazy Horse, defeated Lieutenant George A. Custer and his troops.

★ The mountains within Glacier National Park were carved from prehistoric glaciers, and today the area abounds with natural wonders.

2007 Montana Quarter				
☐ Philadelphia Mint	Acquired from_____	Date: _____	
☐ Denver Mint	Acquired from_____	Date: _____	

Nebraska

Admitted: March 1, 1867 (37th)
Nickname: The Cornhusker State
Capital: Lincoln
Area: 77,358 square miles (16th)
Population: 1.7 million (38th)

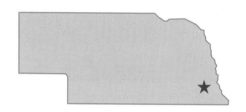

★ Historic Chimney Rock, a tall sandstone steeple in Bayard, was the landmark most frequently mentioned in the diaries of pioneers traveling the Oregon Trail during the 1800s.

★ Archie, the world's largest fossil mammoth, was found near Wellfleet in the early 1900s. He's now on display with other fossils at the University of Nebraska State Museum in Lincoln.

2006 Nebraska Quarter

☐ Philadelphia Mint   Acquired from_____   Date: _____
☐ Denver Mint   Acquired from_____   Date: _____

Nevada

Admitted: October 31, 1864 (36th)
Nickname: The Silver State
Capital: Carson City
Area: 110,567 square miles (7th)
Population: 1.7 million (37th)

★ State Route 375 is known as the "Extraterrestrial Highway" due to the fact that it passes by the secret government military base Area 51, which has long been associated with UFO activity by conspiracy theorists.

★ Nevada's Hoover Dam, built in the 1930s, holds back the waters of Lake Mead, the country's largest artificial reservoir. The amount of concrete used in the building of the dam (the largest of its time) could pave a two-lane highway from New York to San Francisco.

2006 Nevada Quarter

☐ Philadelphia Mint   Acquired from_____   Date: _____
☐ Denver Mint   Acquired from_____   Date: _____

New Hampshire

Admitted: June 21, 1788 (9th)
Nickname: The Granite State
Capital: Concord
Area: 9,283 square miles (44th)
Population: 1.2 million (42nd)

★ Franklin Pierce (1804-1869), the 14th president of the United States, was born in Hillsboro. The Franklin Pierce Homestead is a historic site that is open to visitors.

★ The first free public library in the United States was established at Peterborough in 1833.

★ The first potato ever planted in United States soil was sown at Londonderry Common Field in 1719.

2000 New Hampshire Quarter			
☐ Philadelphia Mint	Acquired from_____	Date: _____	
☐ Denver Mint	Acquired from_____	Date: _____	

New Jersey

Admitted: December 18, 1787 (3rd)
Nickname: The Garden State
Capital: Trenton
Area: 8,215 square miles (46th)
Population: 8.1 million (9th)

★ The country's first drive-in movie theater opened in Camden on June 6, 1933.

★ "Ol' Blue Eyes," Frank Sinatra, was born in Hoboken in 1915. The legendary crooner and actor, who had a lasting impact upon the American entertainment landscape, died on May 14, 1998, at age 82.

★ Thomas Edison, inventor of the phonograph, lightbulb and the motion picture projector, made many of his discoveries at laboratories in Menlo Park and West Orange.

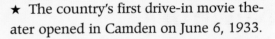

1999 New Jersey Quarter			
☐ Philadelphia Mint	Acquired from_____	Date: _____	
☐ Denver Mint	Acquired from_____	Date: _____	

New Mexico

Admitted: January 6, 1912 (47th)
Nickname: The Land of Enchantment
Capital: Santa Fe
Area: 121,598 square miles (5th)
Population: 1.7 million (36th)

★ White Sands National Monument, located near Alamogordo, is the largest gypsum dune field in the world. The pure white sand dunes, some of which are 60 feet tall, encompass 275 square miles at the northern end of the Chihuahuan Desert.

★ Smokey the Bear, the mascot for the forest fire prevention campaign, was real. He was rescued as a cub from a forest fire and became a living mascot. When Smokey died, he was buried in Capitan, in what is now Smokey Bear Historical State Park.

2008 New Mexico Quarter

☐ Philadelphia Mint   Acquired from_____   Date: _____
☐ Denver Mint   Acquired from_____   Date: _____

New York

Admitted: July 26, 1788 (11th)
Nickname: The Empire State
Capital: Albany
Area: 53,989 square miles (27th)
Population: 18.1 million (3rd)

★ Baseball's greatest moments can be relived at the National Baseball Hall of Fame in Cooperstown. The Hall opened its doors in 1939, when it inducted five players. Today there are well over 200 members of the Hall of Fame, and the building itself houses every conceivable kind of baseball memorabilia.

★ Seneca Falls is home to the Women's Rights National Historic Park. The park commemorates the first-ever Women's Rights Convention, held in Seneca Falls in 1848.

2001 New York Quarter

☐ Philadelphia Mint   Acquired from_____   Date: _____
☐ Denver Mint   Acquired from_____   Date: _____

North Carolina

Admitted: November 21, 1789 (12th)

Nickname: The Tar Heel State

Capital: Raleigh

Area: 52,672 square miles (29th)

Population: 7.4 million (11th)

★ The Wright brothers were "First in Flight" when they took their famous airplane flight into history from Kill Devil Hills, near Kitty Hawk. With Orville at the helm, the first-ever sustained, controlled airplane flight took place on December 17, 1903. It lasted for 12 seconds.

★ Pepsi-Cola was invented in 1898 by a pharmacist in New Bern named Caleb Bradham. The drink, originally called "Brad's drink," was later called Pepsi-Cola because of the pepsin and cola nuts used in the recipe.

2001 North Carolina Quarter

☐ Philadelphia Mint   Acquired from_____   Date: _____

☐ Denver Mint   Acquired from_____   Date: _____

North Dakota

Admitted: November 2, 1889 (39th)

Nickname: The Peace Garden State

Capital: Bismarck

Area: 70,704 square miles (18th)

Population: 640,883 (47th)

★ A golf course spans the international border of Portal, North Dakota and North Portal, Saskatchewan, Canada. The tee for the ninth hole is located in Canada while the hole for the ninth green is located in the United States.

★ Is North Dakota our 39th or 40th state? No one really knows for sure! The day they were admitted to the union, President Benjamin Harrison covered the documents and shuffled them when he signed them, so no one knows which became a state first!

2006 North Dakota Quarter

☐ Philadelphia Mint   Acquired from_____   Date: _____

☐ Denver Mint   Acquired from_____   Date: _____

Ohio

Admitted: February 19, 1803 (17th)
Nickname: The Buckeye State
Capital: Columbus
Area: 44,828 square miles (34th)
Population: 11.2 million (7th)

★ Ohio natives John Glenn and Neil Armstrong are famous for their "firsts." Glenn became the oldest man to travel in space when he flew with *Discovery* in 1998. Thirty-six years earlier, he was the first American to orbit the Earth. Armstrong was the first man to step on the moon in 1969.

★ Seven U.S. Presidents were born in Ohio: Ulysses S. Grant, Rutherford B. Hayes, James A. Garfield, Benjamin Harrison, William McKinley, William Howard Taft and Warren G. Harding.

2002 Ohio Quarter

☐ Philadelphia Mint   Acquired from_____   Date: _____
☐ Denver Mint   Acquired from_____   Date: _____

Oklahoma

Admitted: November 16, 1907 (46th)
Nickname: The Sooner State
Capital: Oklahoma City
Area: 69,903 square miles (20th)
Population: 3.3 million (27th)

★ The Oklahoma state capitol building in Oklahoma City is the only state capitol building in the world with working oil wells on its lawn.

★ Oklahoma is known as the "Sooner" state because of some eager homesteaders during the Land Rush of 1889. In order to stake claim to more desirable land in the Indian Territory, these "sooners" crossed the boundary line sooner than they should have.

2008 Oklahoma Quarter

☐ Philadelphia Mint   Acquired from_____   Date: _____
☐ Denver Mint   Acquired from_____   Date: _____

Oregon

Admitted: February 14, 1859 (33rd)
Nickname: The Beaver State
Capital: Salem
Area: 97,132 square miles (10th)
Population: 3.2 million (29th)

★ You will not be able to find a self-serve gas station in Oregon – it is against the law to pump your own gas in this state.

★ The world's smallest official park is located in Portland and has a total area of 452 square *inches..* Dick Fagan, a local journalist, often wrote about the park and the leprechauns that reportedly congregated there. It became an official park on on St. Patrick's Day, 1948.

2005 Oregon Quarter

☐ Philadelphia Mint   Acquired from_____   Date: _____
☐ Denver Mint   Acquired from_____   Date: _____

Pennsylvania

Admitted: December 12, 1787 (2nd)
Nickname: The Keystone State
Capital: Harrisburg
Area: 46,058 square miles (33rd)
Population: 12 million (5th)

★ The first computer, ENIAC (Electronic Numerical Integrator and Computer), was developed at the University of Pennsylvania in 1946. It wasn't at all like the computers of today – this one weighed more than 30 tons!

★ Batter up! Little League Baseball began in the central Pennsylvania town of Williamsport in 1939.

1999 Pennsylvania Quarter

☐ Philadelphia Mint   Acquired from_____   Date: _____
☐ Denver Mint   Acquired from_____   Date: _____

Rhode Island

Admitted: May 29, 1790 (13th)

Nickname: The Ocean State

Capital: Providence

Area: 1,231 square miles (50th)

Population: 987,429 (43rd)

★ Newport is home to the International Tennis Hall of Fame and Museum, located on the site of the former Newport Casino. The Casino hosted the U.S. National Lawn Tennis Championships (now the U.S. Open) from 1881 until 1915.

★ Rhode Island is home to Touro Synagogue, the nation's oldest synagogue. In 1658, a Jewish congregation was established in Newport, and soon after, in 1763, The Touro Synagogue, designed by noted Colonial architect Peter Harrison, opened its doors.

2001 Rhode Island Quarter

☐ Philadelphia Mint   Acquired from_____   Date: _____

☐ Denver Mint   Acquired from_____   Date: _____

South Carolina

Admitted: May 23, 1788 (8th)

Nickname: The Palmetto State

Capital: Columbia

Area: 31,189 square miles (40th)

Population: 3.8 million (26th)

★ The first battle of the Civil War occurred at Fort Sumter, South Carolina on April 12, 1861. South Carolina was the first state to secede from the Union, several months earlier.

★ The first public museum in the United States is located in Charleston. The Charleston Museum was established in 1773 and continues to operate today.

2000 South Carolina Quarter

☐ Philadelphia Mint   Acquired from_____   Date: _____

☐ Denver Mint   Acquired from_____   Date: _____

South Dakota

Admitted: November 2, 1889 (40th)

Nickname: The Mount Rushmore State

Capital: Pierre

Area: 77,121 square miles (17th)

Population: 737,973 (45th)

★ The Sturgis Rally & Race has been an ongoing tradition for avid motorcyclists since August 1938, when J.C. "Pappy" Hoel, a local motorcycle dealer, organized a two-day riding and racing event in the Black Hills of South Dakota.

★ Mt. Rushmore, the monument of four presidents, was never finished. The sculptor who oversaw the project, Gutzon Borglum, died in 1941, and while the finishing touches were put on the monument, it is still not officially considered complete.

2006 South Dakota Quarter

☐ Philadelphia Mint Acquired from_____ Date: _____

☐ Denver Mint Acquired from_____ Date: _____

Tennessee

Admitted: June 1, 1796 (16th)

Nickname: The Volunteer State

Capital: Nashville

Area: 42,146 square miles (36th)

Population: 5.4 million (17th)

★ "The King of Rock 'n Roll," Elvis Presley, lived in Memphis. His home, Graceland, is now visited by thousands each year. Visitors can also see his famous pink cadillac, as well as all kinds of other Elvis memorabilia.

★ The first periodical devoted to the abolition of slavery, *The Emancipator*, was published in Tennessee in 1820. The writer was resident Elihu Embree.

2002 Tennessee Quarter

☐ Philadelphia Mint Acquired from_____ Date: _____

☐ Denver Mint Acquired from_____ Date: _____

Texas

Admitted: December 29, 1845 (28th)
Nickname: The Lone Star State
Capital: Austin
Area: 267,277 square miles (2nd)
Population: 19.4 million (2nd)

★ At over 266,000 square miles, Texas is the second largest state in the Union, after Alaska.

★ Born in 1907 in Tioga, Gene Autry was the first American singing cowboy, appearing in nearly 100 "horse operas," or musical westerns. His signature song was "Back in the Saddle Again."

★ According to folklore, cowboy Pecos Bill was raised by coyotes in Texas after his parents lost him by the Pecos River.

2004 Texas Quarter

☐ Philadelphia Mint   Acquired from_____   Date: _____
☐ Denver Mint   Acquired from_____   Date: _____

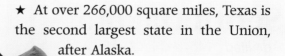

Utah

Admitted: January 4, 1896 (45th)
Nickname: The Beehive State
Capital: Salt Lake City
Area: 84,904 square miles (13th)
Population: 2.1 million (34th)

★ At Four Corners, Utah borders Colorado, New Mexico and Arizona at right angles, the only place in the country that states meet this way. Visitors to this spot can stand on one foot and be in all four states at the same time.

★ Many land speed records have been set at the Bonneville Salt Flats since the world's land speed record of 141 m.p.h. was set in 1914. To date, records of speeds of higher than 600 m.p.h. have been recorded on this naturally straight and perfectly flat surface.

2007 Utah Quarter

☐ Philadelphia Mint   Acquired from_____   Date: _____
☐ Denver Mint   Acquired from_____   Date: _____

Vermont

Admitted: March 4, 1791 (14th)
Nickname: The Green Mountain State
Capital: Montpelier
Area: 9,615 square miles (43rd)
Population: 588,978 (49th)

★ Vermont is the largest producer of maple syrup in the United States. In 1992, it produced a record crop of 570,000 gallons.

★ With fewer than 9,000 residents, Montpelier has the smallest population of any state capital in the United States. It is also the only state capital that is not home to a McDonald's restaurant.

2001 Vermont Quarter

☐ Philadelphia Mint   Acquired from_____   Date: _____
☐ Denver Mint   Acquired from_____   Date: _____

Virginia

Admitted: June 25, 1788 (10th)
Nickname: The Old Dominion State
Capital: Richmond
Area: 42,326 square miles (35th)
Population: 6.7 million (12th)

★ Virginia Democrat L. Douglas Wilder in 1989 became the first elected African American governor in U.S. history.

★ Virginia is home to three natural wonders: Natural Bridge, a stone arch near Lexington that is one of the world's most interesting landforms; Natural Tunnel, an 850-foot-long, 100-foot-high tunnel cut by a creek through a mountain in Scott County; and Natural Chimneys, seven 100-foot-tall towers of rock near Mount Solon.

2000 Virginia Quarter

☐ Philadelphia Mint   Acquired from_____   Date: _____
☐ Denver Mint   Acquired from_____   Date: _____

Washington

Admitted: November 11, 1889 (42nd)
Nickname: The Evergreen State
Capital: Olympia
Area: 70,637 square miles (19th)
Population: 5.6 million (15th)

★ The 607-foot steel Space Needle and a monorail that now connects Seattle Center to downtown Seattle were both built for the 1962 World's Fair.

★ The Columbia River contains one-third of the potential water power in the United States. The Grand Coulee Dam, built on the river in 1941, is one of the greatest power producers in the world.

★ Seattle native and Microsoft executive Bill Gates began programming computers while he was a student in junior high school.

2007 Washington Quarter			
☐ Philadelphia Mint	Acquired from_____	Date: _____	
☐ Denver Mint	Acquired from_____	Date: _____	

West Virginia

Admitted: June 20, 1863 (35th)
Nickname: The Mountain State
Capital: Charleston
Area: 24,231 square miles (41st)
Population: 1.8 million (35th)

★ Born in Myra in 1923, retired Air Force Brigadier General Charles Elwood "Chuck" Yeager became the first person to fly faster than the speed of sound in 1947 in a rocket-powered fighter plane.

★ West Virginia is home to the continent's largest cone-shaped burial mound, Grave Creek Mound, in – appropriately – Moundsville. Built around 250-150 B.C. by the Adena people, the earthen structure is 69 feet tall and consists of multi-level burial tombs. It was discovered in 1838.

2005 West Virginia Quarter			
☐ Philadelphia Mint	Acquired from_____	Date: _____	
☐ Denver Mint	Acquired from_____	Date: _____	

Wisconsin

Admitted: May 29, 1848 (30th)
Nickname: The Badger State
Capital: Madison
Area: 65,499 square miles (22nd)
Population: 5.2 million (18th)

★ Milwaukee printer Christopher Latham Sholes and his associates developed the first practical typewriter in the late 1860s.

★ The nation's first hydroelectric power plant began operating in 1882 in Appleton.

★ Architect Frank Lloyd Wright, considered by many to be one of the greatest architects of the 20th century, was born on June 8, 1867 in Richland Center.

2004 Wisconsin Quarter

__ Philadelphia Mint   Acquired from_____   Date: _____
__ Denver Mint   Acquired from_____   Date: _____

Wyoming

Admitted: July 10, 1890 (44th)
Nickname: The Equality State
Capital: Cheyenne
Area: 97,818 square miles (9th)
Population: 479,743 (50th)

★ In 1869, the Wyoming territorial legislature granted women the right to vote, making them the first women in the nation to have that right.

★ Thousands of pioneers traveling west in the 1800s carved their names on a giant boulder located near Casper that has become known as Independence Rock.

★ Yellowstone National Park, the first and largest National Park in the nation, has most of its acreage in Wyoming.

2007 Wyoming Quarter

__ Philadelphia Mint   Acquired from_____   Date: _____
__ Denver Mint   Acquired from_____   Date: _____

A Closer Look At U.S. Coins

This section explores how each of the six coins in circulation today has changed from its first minting at the end of the 18th century to 21st-century pocket change. Each coin's evolutions are shown, accompanied by a brief historical overview.

Penny

The penny has been in existence since 1793. It originally was just one millimeter smaller than the half dollar and made of copper, but in 1856, legislation was passed to make a smaller coin made of a copper-nickel alloy. In 1909, in honor of the 100th anniversary of Abraham Lincoln's birth, his likeness was added to the obverse of the penny. In 1959, in honor of the 150th anniversary of Lincoln's birth, the Lincoln Memorial was added to the penny's reverse. The penny has maintained the same obverse design longer than any other continually circulating coin.

1793 1793 1793-1796 1796-1807

1808-1814 1816-1839 1839-1857 1856-1858

1859-1909 1909-1958 1959-current

Nickel

The first two nickel designs were issued concurrently. One coin had rays of sunshine on its reverse, while the other coin did not. The next two designs also appeared at the same time, and were made from different metals. One coin's reverse had the word *cents,* while the other coin did not. The original shield on the obverse changed to Lady Liberty in 1883, who maintained her position until 1913. At that time, artist James Earle Fraser, who was well known for "End of the Trail," his world-famous sculpture of an Indian on horseback, was asked by president Theodore Roosevelt to create a new design for the nickel. Fraser created what is now referred to as the "buffalo" nickel (although the creature displayed on the reverse is really a bison). The profile of a proud Indian chief graces the obverse. Twenty-five years later, the U.S. Mint decided to change the design to one that would honor the nation's third president, Thomas Jefferson. A design competition was held and the designer of the winning look was Felix Shlag, who won $1,000 for his effort. His design, which was minted in 1938 and is still in use today, features a profile of Jefferson on the obverse and a frontal view of Jefferson's home, Monticello, on the reverse. Twenty-eight years later, in 1966, Shlag's initials were placed below Jefferson's profile.

| 1866-1883 | 1866-1883 | 1883-1913 | 1883-1913 |

| 1913-1938 | 1913-1938 | 1938-current |

Dime

Early versions of the dime, the quarter, the half dollar and the dollar are all very similar, with Lady Liberty featured on the obverse and an eagle displayed on the reverse. The dime that was used from 1916-1945 is often referred to as the "Mercury" dime, as the obverse features Lady Liberty wearing a winged cap similar to that worn by the mythological winged messenger Mercury. The reverse of this coin depicts a *fasces,* a Roman symbol of authority. The *fasces* is a bundle of sticks, and represents the idea that while a single stick may be easily broken, a group of sticks is much more difficult to break. The axe in the middle of the *fasces* represents military strength. Lady Liberty was replaced by President Franklin Delano Roosevelt in 1946, one year after his death. This dime was created by the chief engraver of the U.S. Mint, John R. Sinnock. The coin features a profile of President Roosevelt on the obverse and a torch (representing liberty) on the reverse, flanked by sprigs of olive (representing peace) and oak (representing strength and independence).

1796-1797   1798-1807   1809-1837   1809-1837

1837-1838   1838-1853, 1855-1860   1853-1855, 1873-1874   1860-1873, 1875-1891

1892-1916   1916-1945   1946-current

Quarter

One of the more famous quarter designs throughout the years is the controversial Standing Liberty design of 1916. Designer Hermon A. MacNeil depicted Lady Liberty with flowing hair and a partially exposed breast. The untamed hair and partial nudity caused an uproar, and one year later, the design was changed to feature Lady Liberty sporting a new hairstyle and less revealing clothing. The quarter that followed was designed by John Flanagan in 1932 to commemorate the 200th anniversary of the birth of George Washington. It was originally intended to serve as a one-year commemorative coin to honor the first president. However, the design was so popular with the public that it soon became a regular-use coin.

1796

1796-1807

1815-1828

1831-1838

1838-1853, 1856-1866

1853

1854-1855

1866-1873, 1875-1891

1873-1874

1892-1916

1916-1917

1917-1930

1932-1975, 1977-1998

1976

1999-2008

Half Dollar

The half dollar suffered from controversy when the Liberty Bell was added to the coin's reverse in 1948. Law requires an eagle to appear on the reverse of all half dollars, so a small eagle was added to the right of the Liberty Bell. The next half dollar design commemorates President John F. Kennedy. The process of creating a new coin design usually takes many months, but the U.S. Mint was able to release the new half dollar just two months after Kennedy's death. The 1964 version of this coin was hoarded by collectors, either in tribute to Kennedy, or because the amount of silver in the coin made it worth more than its face value.

1794-1795	1796-1797	1801-1807	1807-1836
1836-1839	1836-1839	1839-1853, 1856-1866	1853
1854-1855	1866-1873, 1875-1891	1873-1874	1892-1915
1916-1947	1948-1963	1964-1975, 1977-current	1976

Dollar

Since their introduction into U.S. pockets, 15 versions of the dollar coin have been produced by the U.S. Mint. Silver dollars were the first to be minted, the production of which stopped in 1804 and was not resumed until 1840. Gold dollars were authorized in 1849, but their production ended in 1889. A third type of dollar, the trade dollar, made its appearance in 1873. These coins were intended to be used in other countries, but their heaviness made them unpopular. The Dwight D. Eisenhower dollar was released in 1971, followed by the Susan B. Anthony dollar, released in 1979, and the Sacagawea golden dollar, released in 2000.

1794-1795	1795-1804	1795-1804	1840-1873
1840-1873	1849-1854	1854-1856	1856-1889
1873-1885	1878-1921	1921-1935	1971-1975, 1977-1978
1976	1979-1999	2000-current	

Antique Coins

Here is a quick look at the 11 coins that were once used as U.S. currency.

Half Cent (1793-1857): This coin was a failure both for its size and denomination. The public felt it was too bulky and heavy and that it had limited buying power.

Two Cent (1864-1873): Commonly known as "tuppence," this shield-design coin was the first to feature the motto "In God We Trust."

Three Cent (1851-1889): The three-cent coin is the smallest coin produced by the U.S. Mint. It was produced in both nickel and silver. The silver version was more popular, as it was more valuable.

Half Dime (1794-1873): The half dime evolved into the nickel that is used today.

Twenty Cent (1875-1878): Less than 1.5 million of these silver coins were minted, and many of them ended up getting melted for their precious metal, making the twenty-cent piece very hard to find.

Quarter Eagle (1796-1929): This coin, worth $2.50, is thought to have had the largest circulation of any coin in the United States in the 19th century.

Three Dollar (1854-1889): This $3 gold coin was not generally accepted by the public, as many people believed it was unlucky to carry denominations in the number three.

Four Dollar (1879-1880): This $4 gold coin was intended to be used for international purposes. It is commonly known as the "Stella" (the Latin word for *star),* because of the five-pointed star on its reverse.

Half Eagle (1795-1929): The earliest versions of this $5 coin were thought to have been copied from first-century B.C. Roman designs.

Eagle (1795-1933): Many gold eagles, worth $10, were melted, as the value of the gold exceeded the face value of the coin.

Double Eagle (1849-1933): The 1907-1933 version of this $20 coin is widely thought to be the nation's most intricate and beautiful coin. The obverse features a standing Lady Liberty holding the torch of enlightenment in her right hand and an olive branch of peace in her left hand. The reverse shows an eagle soaring high above a rising sun.

Anatomy Of A Dollar Bill

The one-dollar bill, currency that has been in use since 1785, tells an incredible story. The markings found on its face and back reveal bits and pieces of its rich history. Read on for a detailed explanation of all its markings.

The current design on the front of the dollar bill, a portrait of George Washington, was adopted in 1928 (A).

The front of the bill reveals a variety of symbols and numbers. The Federal Reserve seal can be found on the left-hand side of the bill (B). Each Federal Reserve seal contains a letter that represents the Federal

codes). The number of this letter in the alphabet (A=1, F=6 etc.) is also listed four times on the front of the bill (C).

A small letter and number combination is located to the left of the Federal Reserve seal (D). Its official term is "note position letter and quadrant number." It is used to prevent counterfeiting.

Reserve Bank where the bill originated. There are twelve Federal Reserve Banks in all and each is assigned a letter between A and L to identify it (see the box on the next page for a full list of Federal Reserve Bank

A 10-digit serial number can be found on both the lower-left and the upper-right sides of the bill (E). The first letter in this series corresponds with the letter found in the Federal Reserve seal. The letter at the

FEDERAL RESERVE BANK CODES

A 1. . . . . Boston

B 2 . . . . New York

C 3. . . . . Philadelphia

D 4 . . . . : . Cleveland

E 5. . . . . Richmond

F 6. . . . . Atlanta

G 7. . . . . Chicago

H 8 . . . . St. Louis

I 9. . . . . Minneapolis

J 10. . . . . Kansas City

K 11. . . . . Dallas

L 12 . . . . San Francisco

serial number was in the first production run, while a *Z* symbolizes the last run.

The signatures of the Treasurer of the United States (F) and the Secretary of the Treasury (G) appear on every bill (see the box on the next page for a 20-year list of Treasurers of the United States and Secretaries of the Treasury).

Another small letter and number combination appears on the right side of the bill (H). It is officially called the "note position letter and plate serial number," and represents which plate was used to print the bill.

The bill's series year is found on the lower right-hand corner of the front of each dollar bill (I). This represents the year that the bill's design was last changed. If a minor change to the bill is made, such as a

back represents the print run of the bill. For instance, a bill with an *A* at the end of the

new signature, a letter will be added to the end of the series date.

To the right of Washington's portrait is the official seal of the Department of the Treasury (J).

The reverse of the bill features the front of the Great Seal of the United States (1), as well as the back of the Great Seal, an image of an eye above a pyramid (2). The pyramid symbolizes strength and durability, but it is not fully built, signifying the constant growth and improvement of our country. The eye above the pyramid is "all-seeing" and represents divine guidance in America's future. Other features on the reverse of the bill include the phrases "Annuit Coeptis," or "He has favored our undertakings" (3) and "Novus Ordo Seclorum" or "A new order of the ages" (4). The emblem "In God We Trust" was added to the reverse of the bill in 1957 (5).

U.S. TREASURERS 1977-PRESENT

Azie Taylor Morton	1977-1981
Angela Marie Buchanan	1981-1983
Katherine D. Ortega	1983-1989
Catalina Vasquez Villalpando	1989-1993
Mary Ellen Withrow	1994-present

SECRETARIES OF THE TREASURY 1979-PRESENT

G. William Miller	1979-1981
Donald T. Regan	1981-1985
James A. Baker, III	1985-1988
Nicholas F. Brady	1988-1993
Lloyd M. Bentsen	1993-1994
Robert E. Rubin	1995-1999
Lawrence H. Summers	1999-present

Coin Vault – A Look At The Most Valuable U.S. Coins

Are you just starting a collection and wondering which coins you should collect? Read on for some guidelines about which coins are the most valuable to collectors and why.

Coin collectors rely on three major factors to help determine a coin's value: rarity, condition and special circumstances or die varieties.

Rare coins are those that are seen less frequently than others, making them worth more as their demand outweighs their supply. The 1804 U.S. silver dollar is a perfect example of this. Even though these coins were minted in the mid-1830s, they give 1804 as their minting date, as they were produced from an old coin mold. These were the first U.S. coins recognized as rare, and are today one of the most coveted coins among collectors. In 1999, one of these coins sold at auction for more than $4 million.

The condition of a coin also affects its value. This can be determined by grading, a system that rates a coin's condition by analyzing the amount of wear and tear it has experienced. The grading runs from brilliant uncirculated (pristine condition) to poor (badly worn). As a general rule, proof coins (those never entered into circulation) receive the highest values.

A coin also commands a higher value if it has interesting characteristics or major errors. Such coins may have die varieties, such as double die marks or upside down images; rare mint marks; or special metal compositions.

Values fluctuate in the coin market, so if you're buying or selling coins, be sure to deal with a reputable dealer whom you trust.

Behind The Scenes
At The U.S. Mint

Before coins end up in your pocket or in the cash register of the local store, they must be manufactured. It's a multi-stepped process to transform coins from little more than sheet metal to a valuable piece of currency.

The United States coins that fill our pockets, purses and piggy banks are produced under the authority of the U.S. Treasury Department. This department has certainly come a long way since its humble beginnings in 1789 when Alexander Hamilton (whose picture graces the $10 bill) served as the first Secretary of the Treasury.

The U.S. Treasury Department consists of several very important sub-departments ranging from the Internal Revenue Service and the United States Secret Service to the Bureau of Engraving and Printing and the Bureau of the Mint. These departments are directly responsible for the creation of money. The Bureau of Engraving oversees the production of paper currency and the Bureau of the Mint oversees the production of coins.

History Of The U.S. Mint

The U.S. Mint originated as a part of the

Department of State on April 2, 1792. There was just one U.S. Mint at the time, and it was located in Philadelphia. The building occupied by the U.S. Mint has the distinction of being the first building erected by the federal government.

President George Washington named David Rittenhouse the first Director of the U.S. Mint. Rittenhouse, a noted astronomer and instrument maker, held that position until 1795. Some historians believe that President Washington provided some of his very own silver to use in the production of early coins!

The early U.S. Mint was operated quite differently than the one we have today. In the early years, the U.S. Mint's presses were run by human and animal power. Even steam-driven presses were years off!

The U.S. Mint was overseen by the Department of State for more than 80 years. The Coinage Act of 1873, however, re-organized it under the auspices of the Department of the Treasury.

The U.S. Mint Expands

In the mid-1830s, the demand for coins began out-pacing the available supply. To alleviate the problem, Congress authorized the creation of more U.S. Mints, referred to as branch U.S. Mints. These branch U.S. Mints, located in the southern cities of Dahlonega, Georgia, Charlotte, North Carolina and New Orleans, started operating in 1838. A San Francisco Mint followed several years later, in 1852. Various U.S. Mints opened and closed in the following years, primarily because of the fluctuating need for coins.

Today there are branch U.S. Mints in Philadelphia, Denver, San Francisco and West Point, New York. Everyday coins that are used by consumers are produced at the Philadelphia and Denver Mints. The San Francisco Mint produces proofs of coins, while the West Point Mint is largely responsible for manufacturing gold, silver and platinum bullion coins – not circulating currency.

A Coin Is Born

Before the coin-manufacturing process can begin, the necessary supplies have to be purchased. The U.S. Mint buys the raw materials (metals) necessary for coin production from commercial suppliers. The metals arrive in large strips that are about one foot wide and – astoundingly – almost 2,000 feet long. Each huge strip is just a fraction of the total number that the U.S. Mint needs to produce the almost 20 billion coins entered into circulation every year.

In the first step of the production process, the strips of metal are processed through a machine called a blanking press. The blanking press acts like a giant paper punch, popping out blank disks, called planchets, to be made into coins.

This process does not occur, however, with one-cent pieces. For these coins, the U.S. Mint receives already-formed blanks made of copper and zinc directly from its distributors. The remainder of the process stays the same.

The blank planchets then need to go through a cleaning process. They are first placed in an annealing furnace that softens the blank planchets by heating them. Then, just like you do with your dirty laundry, they are placed in a washer. But these washing machines don't use regular laundry detergent. They use chemicals as a cleanser to give the blank planchets a bright and shiny appearance.

In the next step, misshapen and missized blank planchets are weeded out by a machine called a riddler. The step after that is reserved for nickel and penny blank planchets only, which get passed through an upsetting mill. The upsetting mill thickens and raises the edges of these coins.

The coinage presses are the last stop for the fledgling coins. They stamp the obverse and the reverse markings onto the coin in one quick step.

A combination of human power and machines ensure that the finished coins meet all quality standards. A press operator is responsible for visually inspecting each new batch of coins. A coin-sizer machine acts as the final safeguard and weeds out all of the less-than-perfect coins.

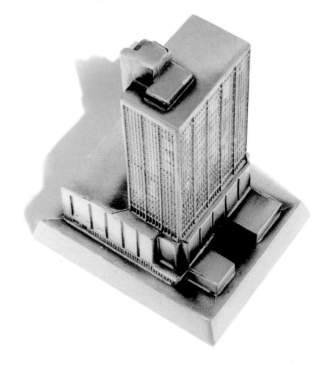

How The Federal Reserve Banks Figure In

The new coins are now ready to go into circulation. The U.S. Mint sends them to the 12 Federal Reserve Banks located

throughout the country for distribution. This journey can be made through the mail, although many coins arrive in style in armored trucks. The Federal Reserve Banks buy the coins they receive and pay the U.S. Treasury face value for them. The Federal Reserve Banks then distribute the coins to the country's commercial depository banks. Commercial depository banks are the ones you go to whenever you need money.

In addition to distributing money to commercial depository banks, the Federal Reserve Banks take in the excess money depository banks accumulate (there are limits as to how much cash commercial depository banks can have on hand). This money is saved in a special account within the nearest Federal Reserve Bank.

Another responsibility of the Federal Reserve Banks is to set U.S. monetary policy. These policies are intended to stimulate the economy while at the same time keeping prices stable. To meet this goal, the Federal Reserve Banks affect the amount of money in the depository banks' reserves.

Although estimating the need for coinage is an inexact science, the U.S. Mint bases its production numbers on seasonal demands and previous-year indicators. Once the U.S. Mint meets its production goals, no more coins are produced for that year. Only if an emergency arises do the presses start rolling again.

Old Coins Never Die... They Get Recycled!

Although the State Quarters will be flooding the cash drawers of banks and businesses for the next 10 years, that does not mean that the original eagle quarters will vanish anytime soon. Coins have an approximate life span of 25 years. They are only removed from circulation if they become uncurrent or mutilated.

An uncurrent coin is one that is worn out but still identifiable and able to be counted by a machine. Uncurrent coins get sent to the Federal Reserve Banks, which send them to the U.S. Mint for recycling.

Mutilated coins are in much worse shape than uncurrent coins and have suffered far more than just normal wear. Coins are considered mutilated if they are unable to be read by a machine. This can mean they are cracked, welded together, bent or otherwise broken. Mutilated coins go straight to the U.S. Mint for recycling.

The U.S. Mint melts down all uncurrent and mutilated coins for future use. This allows for the continuation of the coin manufacturing cycle because these melted coins are recycled into the strips from which future coins will be made.

Funding The State Quarter Program

Happily, the State Quarters program is being financed at no cost to taxpayers. A quarter costs only five cents to produce, so when the Federal Reserve Banks pay face value for the quarters they buy, the government receives a profit of 20 cents for every quarter made. With an estimated five billion quarters being produced each year during the State Quarters program's duration, the U.S. Treasury stands to reap a profit of approximately $10 billion. Even after subtracting out all the necessary expenses of creating the new quarters, a tidy sum stands to remain for the U.S. Treasury, funds that perhaps can be used for new and exciting projects such as the State Quarters program.

Coin Collecting 101

The State Quarters program has gotten many people started as numismatists. Are you a numismatist? If you collect coins, paper money, medals or tokens, then the answer is yes, you are a numismatist! Read on to learn more about this interesting and educational pursuit.

C oins are among the most popular fields of study in numismatics. Coin collecting is a popular hobby because it offers limitless possibilities in the ways you can go about assembling your collection. Whether you have an interest in old and valuable coins, or simply enjoy the challenge of sorting through your loose pocket change in search of the latest State Quarter, coin collecting can be a rewarding hobby for any budget or experience level.

What To Collect

Before you start an "official" coin collection, look over the coins you've already assembled or put some thought into what kinds of coins you'd like to collect. Most collectors either collect by series or by type. This limits you from buying anything and everything, and gives your collection a solid focus and foundation, should you choose to expand it.

A "series" collector focuses on a specific coin. This collector strives to amass all the dates, mint marks and design changes of that particular coin. For example, a Lincoln cent series collection would begin with  the coin's introduction in 1909, and would include such design and composition changes as the 1943 steel cent, the first Lincoln Memorial reverse in 1959 and the 1972 double-die error.

A "type" collector is only interested in obtaining one coin from each series of a particular time period. This time period can be broad, such as 18th Century Colonial coins, or narrow, like U.S. coins of the 1950s. And remember, you do not need to limit yourself to collecting coins only from the United States. Countries all over the world issue currency that in most cases can be obtained with little difficulty by curious collectors.

Supplies

While you probably don't want to store a valuable coin collection in bags or boxes, these simple supplies can be quite effective in protecting a basic coin collection. Investing in storage supplies for more valuable coins, however, is a wise choice. Folders, mounts, tubes and albums are just some of the holders available for displaying your coins. A popular kind of holder is the plastic "flip" holder. It provides a safe and convenient way to examine your coins and quickly flip through them.

Whenever you buy any coin supplies made of plastic, however, be aware that some plastics are not recommended for longtime storage. Products containing polyvinyl chlorides (PVCs), for instance, should not be used for long-term storage as they can leave a green deposit that might stain your coins.

You can find supplies with relative ease in varying degrees of quality and price at your local coin shop.

Grading And Condition

If you plan on purchasing some or all of your coin collection, it is smart to have a rough idea on how coins are graded, or assigned value. As a general rule of thumb, coins in better condition are worth more than coins in lesser condition.

There is a range of terms to describe coin conditions, which range from poor/fair to uncirculated or mint. Flawless, uncirculated coins are the finest specimens available. In some instances they can sell for multiple times what an almost-perfect "about uncirculated" can. Remember, though, that condition is subjective. One dealer's "fine" coin may only be seen as "good" by another.

If you are curious to know the value of the coins you already have, you might want to have them "slabbed." Slabbing is a popular trend in the field of grading. You send your coins to an independent grading service that assigns value to them. The grading service sonically seals your coins in individual non-PVC plastic and certifies them with all their pertinent information clearly labeled on the slab. Keep in mind that slabbing can be expensive, and might be cost-prohibitive for some coins.

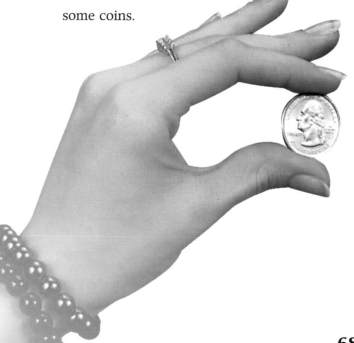

Eye appeal is a very important factor in grading a coin. Blemishes to look out for when buying a coin include worn dates and letters. Severely tarnished coins may also be considered unattractive to some collectors. It is important to never clean your coins, no matter how dirty or tarnished they are. Many collectors prefer a true appearance than an artificially shiny coin. If any cleaning is to be done, it should only be done by a professional. A coin that has been cleaned by a novice can typically see its value plummet.

When handling and inspecting your coins, always hold the coin along the rim by its edges. Placing your fingers on the obverse or the reverse can leave fingerprints and contribute to wear.

Where To Buy Your Coins

Unless you are collecting only relatively current and circulating coins, you will probably need to purchase your coins. Check your phone book for dealers in your area. Talk with other collectors to find out who the best and most reputable dealers are.

How do you find these other collectors? Consider joining a coin club. There are small, local clubs all over the country, as well as national groups such as the American Numismatic Association and the American Numismatic Society.

If you find these options limiting, then the Internet can put you in contact with dealers and collectors from all over the country.

What Is My Collection Worth?

If you are planning to pay for your child's college education with your State Quarter collection, you might want to reconsider. With billions of State Quarters produced each year, the chances are slim that they will see a dramatic increase in value. Keep your eyes open, however, for errors or variations in the quarters that may raise their value on the secondary market.

Errors such as a blank planchet, a clipped planchet and off-center coins occur during the minting process and are often prized by collectors and serve as interesting conversation pieces.

The same advice holds true for older coins and paper money as well. With the exception of particular years and mint marks, many coins from the early 20th century in good or fine condition can be bought for low prices. Even if your coin collection is not particularly valuable, the sense of history one experiences when interacting with these old coins is often reward enough.

Terminology

Has all the numismatic lingo confused you? This listing of terms and phrases often used by coin collectors should help you.

Barber coins – short for Charles Barber, designer of the "Barber" dime (1892-1916), quarter (1892-1916) and half dollar (1892-1915)

blank planchet error – an unstruck planchet that has passed through inspection undetected

bullion coins – coins minted from the precious metals gold, silver and platinum

circulating – a coin that changes hands through normal routes of commerce

clad – coin made from different metals that have been bonded together

clipped planchet – an error resulting in a coin having a partially clipped appearance (partially cut off)

die – a steel cylinder used to strike the obverse and reverse designs on a coin

double die – a die error resulting in a coin's design appearing doubled

error – a mistake to a coin that often occurs during the minting process

grade – the condition of a coin

mint marks – small letters on a coin that denote which U.S. Mint produced it

numismatic – one who collects coins, paper money, medals or tokens

obverse – the front or "heads" surface of a coin

off-center – error causing the coin design to miss being stamped in the center

planchet – a flat, blank disk that has not been struck

proof – a coin that has been given a mirror-like finish during a special minting process

reverse – the back or "tails" surface of a coin

rim – the raised ridge along a coin that prevents wear

strike – to imprint a blank coin with its design during the minting process

uncirculated – a coin that has avoided usage; exhibits no normal wear

wear – erosion of detail to a coin

State Quarters
Chronological Checklist

Use this checklist to keep track of which quarters you have and which ones you still need to find. *P* stands for Philadelphia Mint and *D* stands for Denver Mint. The quarters are being released in the order in which the states signed the Constitution and joined the Union. Dates of admission are in parentheses.

1999
P D
- ❏ ❏ Delaware (December 7, 1787)
- ❏ ❏ Pennsylvania (December 12, 1787)
- ❏ ❏ New Jersey (December 18, 1787)
- ❏ ❏ Georgia (January 2, 1788)
- ❏ ❏ Connecticut (January 9, 1788)

2000
P D
- ❏ ❏ Massachusetts (February 6, 1788)
- ❏ ❏ Maryland (April 28, 1788)
- ❏ ❏ South Carolina (May 23, 1788)
- ❏ ❏ New Hampshire (June 21, 1788)
- ❏ ❏ Virginia (June 25, 1788)

2001
P D
- ❏ ❏ New York (July 26, 1788)
- ❏ ❏ North Carolina (November 21, 1789)
- ❏ ❏ Rhode Island (May 29, 1790)
- ❏ ❏ Vermont (March 4, 1791)
- ❏ ❏ Kentucky (June 1, 1792)

2002
P D
- ❏ ❏ Tennessee (June 1, 1796)
- ❏ ❏ Ohio (February 19, 1803)
- ❏ ❏ Louisiana (April 30, 1812)
- ❏ ❏ Indiana (December 11, 1816)
- ❏ ❏ Mississippi (December 10, 1817)

2003
P D
- ❏ ❏ Illinois (December 3, 1818)
- ❏ ❏ Alabama (December 14, 1819)
- ❏ ❏ Maine (March 15, 1820)
- ❏ ❏ Missouri (August 10, 1821)
- ❏ ❏ Arkansas (June 15, 1836)

2004
P D
- ❏ ❏ Michigan (January 26, 1837)
- ❏ ❏ Florida (March 3, 1845)
- ❏ ❏ Texas (December 29, 1845)
- ❏ ❏ Iowa (December 28, 1846)
- ❏ ❏ Wisconsin (May 29, 1848)

2005
P D
- ❏ ❏ California (September 9, 1850)
- ❏ ❏ Minnesota (May 11, 1858)
- ❏ ❏ Oregon (February 14, 1859)
- ❏ ❏ Kansas (January 29, 1861)
- ❏ ❏ West Virginia (June 20, 1863)

2006
P D
- ❏ ❏ Nevada (October 31, 1864)
- ❏ ❏ Nebraska (March 1, 1867)
- ❏ ❏ Colorado (August 1, 1876)
- ❏ ❏ North Dakota (November 2, 1889)
- ❏ ❏ South Dakota (November 2, 1889)

2007
P D
- ❏ ❏ Montana (November 8, 1889)
- ❏ ❏ Washington (November 11, 1889)
- ❏ ❏ Idaho (July 3, 1890)
- ❏ ❏ Wyoming (July 10, 1890)
- ❏ ❏ Utah (January 4, 1896)

2008
P D
- ❏ ❏ Oklahoma (November 16, 1907)
- ❏ ❏ New Mexico (January 6, 1912)
- ❏ ❏ Arizona (February 14, 1912)
- ❏ ❏ Alaska (January 3, 1959)
- ❏ ❏ Hawaii (August 21, 1959)